The Best Authentic

Australian Cookbook

Australian Recipes for a Fancy Meal with Family

By

Angel Burns

License Notices

This book or parts thereof might not be reproduced in any format for personal or commercial use without the written permission of the author. Possession and distribution of this book by any means without said permission is prohibited by law.

All content is for entertainment purposes and the author accepts no responsibility for any damages, commercially or personally, caused by following the content.

Get Your Daily Deals Here!

Free books on me! Subscribe now to receive free and discounted books directly to your email. This means you will always have choices of your next book from the comfort of your own home and a reminder email will pop up a few days beforehand, so you never miss out! Every day, free books will make their way into your inbox and all you need to do is choose what you want.

What could be better than that?

Fill out the box below to get started on this amazing offer and start receiving your daily deals right away!

https://angel-burns.gr8.com

Table of Contents

Authentic Australian Recipes

HHHHHHHHHHHHHHHHHHHHHHHHHHHHHHHHHHHHHHHHH

Recipe 1: Australian Vanilla Slice

This is the perfect dish for you to make whenever you are craving something on the sweet side. It will satisfy the strongest sweet tooth.

Yield: 16 servings

Preparation Time: 6 hours and 25 minutes

Ingredient List:

- 1 pack of puff pastry
- 2 cups of whole milk
- 2 cups of half and half
- 1 cup of white sugar
- ¾ cup of cornstarch
- ½ cup of vanilla pudding
- 3 egg yolks
- 1 tablespoon of pure vanilla
- 4 Tablespoons of butter, soft
- Powdered sugar, for dusting

HHHHHHHHHHHHHHHHHHHHHHHHHHHHHHHHHHHHH

Instructions:

1. Preheat the oven to 400 degrees. Place a sheet of parchment paper onto a baking sheet.

2. Place the puff pastry sheets onto the baking sheet. Piece with a fork over the surface.

3. Place into the oven to bake for 15 to 20 minutes or until golden. Remove and set aside to cool completely.

4. Add a sheet of aluminum foil into a baking dish. Press one of the baked puff pastries into the bottom of the baking dish.

5. In a saucepan set over medium to high heat, add in the milk. Allow to come to a simmer. Add in the half and half, white sugar, cornstarch, pudding and egg yolks. Whisk until smooth in consistency. Cook for 2 minutes or until thick in consistency. Remove from heat. Add in the pure vanilla and soft butter. Stir well to mix. Pour into the baking dish.

6. Add the second puff pastry sheet over the top. Press down gently.

7. Cover and place into the fridge to chill for 6 hours.

8. Dust with powdered sugar. Slice and serve.

Recipe 2: Australian Lime Pie

This is the perfect pie dish to serve to your family whenever you want to spoil your friends and family with something sweet.

Yield: 8 servings

Preparation Time:1 hour and 35 minutes

Ingredient List:

- 2/3 cup of rolled oats
- 2/3 cup of coconut, flaked
- 2/3 cup of all-purpose flour
- ½ cup of white sugar
- ½ cup of butter, melted
- 2 Tablespoons of light corn syrup
- 1 teaspoon of baking soda
- 1, 14 ounce can of sweet condensed milk
- ½ cup of lime juice
- 4 egg yolks, beaten
- 2 teaspoons of grated lemon zest

HHHHHHHHHHHHHHHHHHHHHHHHHHHHHHHHHHHHH

Instructions:

1. Preheat the oven to 350 degrees. Grease a pie pan with cooking spray.

2. In a bowl, add in the rolled oats, flaked coconut, all-purpose flour and white sugar. Stir well to mix.

3. In a separate bowl, add in the melted butter, corn syrup and baking soda. Beat with an electric mixer until frothy. Add in the oat mix and stir well until just mixed.

4. Pour into the pie pan.

5. In a bowl, add in the condensed milk, lime juice, beaten egg yolks and lemon rind. Beat with an electric mixer until mixed. Pour into the pie pan.

6. Place into the oven to bake for 20 minutes or until firm.

7. Remove and cover. Set into the fridge to chill for 1 hour.

8. Slice and serve.

Recipe 3: Classic Lamingtons

Australian lamingtons are sponge cakes coated in decadent chocolate and grated coconut to make a dish that is impossible to say no to.

Yield: 24 servings

Preparation Time: 1 day, 1 hour and 55 minutes

Ingredients for the cake:

- 2 cups of all-purpose flour
- 4 teaspoons of baker's style baking powder
- Dash of salt
- ½ cup of butter, soft
- ¾ cup of white sugar
- 1 teaspoon of pure vanilla
- 2 eggs
- ½ cup of whole milk

Ingredients for the icing:

- 4 cups of powdered sugar
- 1/3 cup of powdered cocoa
- 2 Tablespoons of butter, melted
- ½ cup of whole milk
- 1 pounds of unsweetened coconut, dried

HHHHHHHHHHHHHHHHHHHHHHHHHHHHHHHHHHHHHHH

Instructions:

1. Preheat the oven to 375 degrees. Grease a baking dish and dust lightly with flour.

2. Prepare the cake. In a bowl, add in the all-purpose flour, dash of salt and baking powder. Stir well to mix and set aside.

3. In a separate bowl, add in the butter and white sugar. Beat with an electric mixer until fluffy in consistency. Add in the eggs, pure vanilla, whole milk and flour mix. Continue to beat until just mixed.

4. Pour into the baking dish.

5. Place into the oven to bake for 35 to 40 minutes or until baked through. Remove and set aside to cool completely.

6. Prepare the icing. In a bowl, add in the powdered sugar, powdered cocoa and melted butter. Beat with an electric mixer until smooth in consistency.

7. Slice the cake into squares. Dip the squares into the icing. Sprinkle the dried coconut over the top of the squares.

8. Serve.

Recipe 4: Australian Rissoles

This is a delicious dish you can make whenever you want to make an authentic Australian meal in the comfort of your own home.

Yield: 15 servings

Preparation Time:20 minutes

Ingredient List:

- 1 pound of lean ground beef
- 1 onion, chopped
- 1 cup of breadcrumbs
- ½ teaspoons of dried basil
- 1 tablespoon of parsley, chopped
- 1 egg, beaten
- All-purpose flour, as needed

HHHHHHHHHHHHHHHHHHHHHHHHHHHHHHHHHHHHHH

Instructions:

1. In a bowl, add in the lean beef, chopped onion, breadcrumbs, dried basil, chopped parsley and egg. Stir well to mix.

2. Shape into balls and flatten the balls slightly.

3. Place 1 cup of flour into a Ziploc bag. Add in the rissoles and toss to coat.

4. Place onto a preheated grill. Cook for 8 to 10 minutes or until cooked through.

5. Remove and serve immediately.

Recipe 5: Australian Miniature Beef Pies

These miniature beef pies are essential in most Australian households today. They are enjoyed by both children and adults of all ages.

Yield: 16 servings

Preparation Time:50 minutes

Ingredients for the filling:

- 3 Tablespoons of extra virgin olive oil
- 3 pounds of chuck steak, cut into small cubes
- 2 onions, peeled and chopped
- 3 cloves of garlic, minced
- 2 Tablespoons of tomato paste
- 4 cups of beef stock
- 1 cup of dried red wine
- 2 bay leaves, dried
- 1 ½ teaspoons of salt
- 2 teaspoons of black pepper
- 3 Tablespoons of cornstarch
- 4 Tablespoons of water

Ingredients for the pastry:

- 1 egg yolk, beaten
- 4 sheets of short crust pastry
- 3 to 4 sheets of puff pastry

HHHHHHHHHHHHHHHHHHHHHHHHHHHHHHHHHHHHHHH

Instructions:

1. Prepare the filling. In a pot set over high heat, add in 1 tablespoon of olive oil. Add in the beef and cook for 5 minutes or until seared on all sides. Transfer into a bowl and set aside.

2. Lower the heat to medium and add in the remaining extra virgin olive oil. Add in the chopped onions and minced garlic. Cook for 5 minutes or until soft.

3. Add in the beef back into the pot. Add in the tomato paste, beef stock, dried red wine, dried bay leaves, cornstarch and water. Season with a dash of salt and black pepper. Stir well to mix. Allow to come to a simmer. Lower the heat to low and allow to cook for 50 minutes to 1 hour or until the beef is soft. Remove from heat and set aside to cool slightly.

4. Preheat the oven to 350 degrees. Grease a muffin pan with cooking spray.

5. Use a 4 inch cookie cutter and cut out rounds from the short crust pastry. Place into the muffin cups.

6. Pour the filling into the muffin cups.

7. Use a 3 inch cookie cutter and cut out rounds from the puff pastry. Place over the top of the filling. Pierce with a knife for venting.

8. Brush with the beaten egg yolk.

9. Place into the oven to bake for 20 to 25 minutes or until golden.

10. Remove and set aside to rest for 10 minutes before serving.

Recipe 6: Orange Cake

This is a moist cake you can make whenever you need something sweet to spoil your friends and family with. It is so delicious, you will want to make it every day.

Yield: 12 servings

Preparation Time: 1 hour

Ingredient List:

- ¾ cup of caster sugar
- 1 ½ cups of self-rising flour
- 2 eggs, beaten
- 1 orange, zest and juice only
- ½ cups of whole milk
- 4 Tablespoons of butter, melted

Ingredients for the icing:

- 2 cups of powdered sugar
- 2 Tablespoons of orange juice

HHHHHHHHHHHHHHHHHHHHHHHHHHHHHHHHHHHHHH

Instructions:

1. Preheat the oven to 350 degrees. Grease a loaf pan with cooking spray. Dust lightly flour.

2. In a bowl, add in the caster sugar, self-rising flour, beaten eggs, fresh orange zest and fresh orange juice. Add in ½ cup of whole milk. Whisk well until just mixed.

3. Pour into the loaf pan.

4. Place into the oven to bake for 35 to 40 minutes or until baked through. Remove and set aside to cool for 5 minutes.

5. Prepare the icing. In a bowl, add in the powdered sugar and orange juice. Whisk until smooth in consistency. Pour over the top of the loaf.

6. Allow the loaf to rest for 10 minutes or until the icing is set.

7. Slice and serve.

Recipe 7: Zucchini Slice

This is a healthy and savory Australian appetizer dish that is perfect to make for any occasion. Serve as a tasty appetizer during your next dinner event.

Yield: 12 servings

Preparation Time: 55 minutes

Ingredient List:

- 3 cups of zucchini, grated and drained
- 3 slices of Applewood bacon, chopped
- 1 red onion, chopped
- 5 eggs
- ½ cup of extra virgin olive oil
- Dash of black pepper
- 1 cup of all-purpose flour
- 2 teaspoons of baking powder
- 2/3 cup of goat cheese, crumbled

HHHHHHHHHHHHHHHHHHHHHHHHHHHHHHHHHHHHHH

Instructions:

1. Preheat the oven to 350 degrees. Add a sheet of parchment paper into a baking dish. Grease with cooking spray.

2. In a bowl, add in the grated zucchini.

3. In a skillet set over low to medium heat, add in the chopped bacon. Cook for 3 minutes or until browned. Add in the chopped red onion. Cook for 5 minutes or until soft.

4. In a separate bowl, add in the eggs and olive oil. Season with salt and black pepper. Whisk until lightly beaten. Add in the cooked onion mix and grated zucchini. Stir well to incorporate. Add in the all-purpose flour and baking powder. Stir well to mix.

5. Pour into the baking dish. Sprinkle the crumbled goat cheese over the top.

6. Place into the oven to bake for 45 to 50 minutes or until set.

7. Remove and cool for 10 minutes before serving.

Recipe 8: Potato Roast

This is a dish that will stun your friends and family. It is absolutely delicious and makes for the perfect side dish to serve during your next meal.

Yield: 4 servings

Preparation Time: 1 hour and 30 minutes

Ingredient List:

- 3 Tablespoons of butter, melted
- 3 Tablespoons of extra virgin olive oil
- 10 to 12 russet potatoes, peeled
- Dash of salt
- 1 onion, thinly sliced
- ½ teaspoons of crushed red pepper flakes
- 6 sprigs of thyme
- 3 ounces of pancetta, cut into cubes and cooked

HHHHHHHHHHHHHHHHHHHHHHHHHHHHHHHHHHHHHHHH

Instructions:

1. Preheat the oven to 375 degrees.

2. In a bowl, add in the olive oil and melted butter. Stir well to mix. Set aside.

3. Grease a round baking dish with a bit of the butter mix.

4. Slice the potato slices thinly. Place into the baking dish. Season with a dash of salt and crushed red pepper flakes. Brush with the remaining butter mix.

5. Place into the oven to bake for 1 hour and 25 minutes.

6. Sprinkle the cubes of pancetta and thyme sprigs over the potatoes.

7. Serve immediately.

Recipe 9: Australian Honey Joys

This is a classic Australian recipe often made as a treat for kids parties. It is incredibly easy to make and can be made in just a few minutes.

Yield: 4 servings

Preparation Time: 15 minutes

Ingredient List:

- 6 Tablespoons of butter, soft
- ¼ cup of white sugar
- 2 Tablespoons of honey
- 4 cups of cornflakes

HHHHHHHHHHHHHHHHHHHHHHHHHHHHHHHHHHHHHH

Instructions:

1. Preheat the oven to 300 degrees. Place paper muffin liners into a greased muffin pan.

2. In a saucepan set over medium heat, add in the butter. Allow to melt. Add in the white sugar and honey. Stir well until frothy.

3. Add in the cornflakes and removed from heat. Stir well until coated.

4. Spoon into the muffin pan.

5. Place into the oven to bake for 10 minutes.

6. Remove and cool for 5 minutes before serving.

Recipe 10: Vegemite and Cheese Rolls

These rolls are perfect to make regardless of the occasion. I guarantee everybody in your home with adore these rolls.

Yield: 8 servings

Preparation Time: 30 minutes

Ingredient List:

- 1 ½ cups of self-rising flour
- ½ cup of all-purpose flour
- 2 Tablespoons of butter
- 2/3 cup of whole milk
- ½ cup of cheddar cheese
- ¼ cup of parmesan cheese
- 1 tablespoon of Vegemite
- 1 tablespoon of whole milk

HHHHHHHHHHHHHHHHHHHHHHHHHHHHHHHHHHHHHHHH

Instructions:

1. Preheat the oven to 390 degrees.

2. In a bowl, add in the self rising and all-purpose flour. Add in the butter and stir well to mix.

3. Add in the cheddar cheese, parmesan cheese and 2/3 cup of whole milk. Stir well until a dough begins to form.

4. Knead the dough on a flat surface until smooth in consistency. Roll the dough into a rectangle that is 1 inch in thickness.

5. Spread the Vegemite over the top of the dough. Sprinkle a dash of Parmesan cheese and cheddar cheese over the top.

6. Roll the dough into a log. Slice into 8 rolls and place onto a baking sheet.

7. Brush the rolls with the remaining milk.

8. Place into the oven to bake for 20 minutes.

9. Remove and cool for 5 minutes before serving.

Recipe 11: Australian Mince and Pot Hot Pot

This is a very filling and delicious Australian dish that is perfect to serve during any night of the week. It is so filling, it will leave you feeling full for hours.

Yield: 6 servings

Preparation Time: 1 hour and 15 minutes

Ingredient List:

- 5 potatoes, peeled and sliced
- 1 tablespoon of extra virgin olive oil
- 1 pound of lean ground beef
- 1 onion, chopped
- 1 tablespoon of tomato sauce
- 1 tablespoon of Worcestershire sauce
- Dash of salt and black pepper
- ¼ cup of butter
- ¼ cup of all-purpose flour
- 2 cups of whole milk
- 1 cup of sharp cheddar cheese, shredded
- 1, 6 ounce can of mushrooms, drained
- 2 Tablespoons of butter, chopped

HHHHHHHHHHHHHHHHHHHHHHHHHHHHHHHHHHHHHH

Instructions:

1. Preheat the oven to 350 degrees.

2. In a bowl, add in the slices of potatoes. Cover with water and set aside to soak.

3. In a saucepan set over medium heat, add in the olive oil. Add in the ground beef, chopped onion, tomato sauce and Worcestershire sauce. Season with a dash of salt and black pepper. Cook for 8 to 10 minutes or until soft.

4. In a saucepan set over medium heat, add in ¼ cup of butter. Allow to melt. Add in the all-purpose flour and whisk until smooth in consistency. Add in the whole milk. Cook for 5 minutes or until thick in consistency.

5. Lower the heat to low. Add in the shredded sharp cheddar cheese. Season with a dash of salt and black pepper.

6. Drain the potato slices. In a baking dish, add in the potato slices. Pour the beef mix over the potato slices and top off with the canned mushrooms. Cover with the cheese mix. Dot with 2 tablespoons of butter.

7. Place into the oven to bake for 35 to 40 minutes or until browned.

8. Remove and serve immediately.

Recipe 12: Australian Burgers

Make this delicious Australian dish whenever you are craving burgers. Feel free to top these burgers off with your favorite toppings.

Yield: 3 servings

Preparation Time: 25 minutes

Ingredient List:

- 3 pounds of lean ground beef
- 1 teaspoon of crushed red pepper flakes
- 1 teaspoon of powdered garlic
- 1 teaspoon of salt
- Dash of black pepper
- 1, 14 ounce can of pineapple rings
- ¼ cup of ketchup
- ¼ cup of mayonnaise
- 1 teaspoon of Asian chili paste
- 2 Tablespoons of vegetable oil, evenly divided
- 4 eggs, cooked skinny side up
- 1, 8 ounce can of pickled beets, thinly sliced
- 4 slices of cheddar cheese
- 1 onion, thinly sliced and sautéed
- 4 hamburger buns

HHHHHHHHHHHHHHHHHHHHHHHHHHHHHHHHHHHHHHH

Instructions:

1. In a bowl, add in the ground beef, crushed red pepper flakes and powdered garlic. Season with a dash of salt and black pepper. Shape into 4 patties that are 1 inch in size.

2. Place a cast iron skillet over medium to high heat. Grease with 1 tablespoon of canola oil. Brush the pineapple rings with oil. Place into the skillet. Cook for 2 minutes on each side or until seared. Remove and set aside.

3. Add the burger patties. Cook for 10 minutes on each side or until cooked through.

4. Top off with the slices of cheese. Allow the cheese to melt completely.

5. Transfer onto the burger buns.

6. In a bowl, add in the ketchup, mayonnaise and Asian chili paste. Stir well to mix.

7. Top off the burgers with the cooked eggs, sliced beets, sliced onion, pineapple rings and chili mayo.

8. Serve immediately.

Recipe 13: Classic Australian Sausage Rolls

Whenever you think of Australia, the first type of food to pop into mind is the sausage rolls. Freshly made sausage wrapped in a flaky pastry, what is there not to love?

Yield: 8 servings

Preparation Time: 55 minutes

Ingredient List:

- 16 ounces of pork sausage
- 1 pack of puff pastry
- ¾ cup of Italian breadcrumbs
- 1/3 cup of whole milk
- 1 teaspoon of garlic, minced
- ½ teaspoons of smoked paprika
- Dash of salt and black pepper

Ingredients for the egg wash:

- 1 egg
- 1 tablespoon of water

HHHHHHHHHHHHHHHHHHHHHHHHHHHHHHHHHHHHHH

Instructions:

1. Preheat the oven to 425 degrees.

2. Place the puff pastry onto a lightly floured surface. Slice the squares into 4 rectangles.

3. In a bowl, add in the pork sausage, Italian breadcrumbs, whole milk, minced garlic and smoked paprika. Season with a dash of salt and black pepper. Stir well until incorporated. Divide among the dough rectangles.

4. Roll the puff pastry over the filling and pinch the edges to seal together. Slice into 4 pieces. Transfer onto a baking sheet.

5. Prepare the egg wash. In a bowl, add in the egg and water. Whisk until lightly beaten. Brush onto the rolls.

6. Place into the oven to bake for 5 minutes. Lower the heat of the oven to 350 degrees. Continue to bake for 30 to 35 minutes or until golden. Set aside to cool.

7. Remove and cool for 5 minutes before serving.

Recipe 14: Pork Chops in Raspberry Sauce

This is the perfect Australian dish for you to make whenever you want to impress your friends and family with your Australian cooking skills.

Yield: 4 servings

Preparation Time:30 minutes

Ingredient List:

- ½ teaspoons of dried thyme
- ½ teaspoons of dried sage
- ¼ teaspoons of salt
- ¼ teaspoons of black pepper
- 4, 4 ounces pork chops, boneless
- 1 tablespoon of butter
- 1 tablespoon of extra virgin olive oil
- ¼ cup of raspberry jam, seedless
- 2 Tablespoons of orange juice
- 2 Tablespoons of white wine vinegar
- 4 sprigs of thyme

HHHHHHHHHHHHHHHHHHHHHHHHHHHHHHHHHHHHHHH

Instructions:

1. Preheat the oven to 200 degrees.

2. In a bowl, add in the dried thyme, dried sage, dash of salt and black pepper. Stir well to mix. Rub this mix over the pork chops.

3. In a skillet set over medium heat, add in the butter and extra virgin olive oil. Add in the pork chops. Cook for 5 minutes on each side or until cooked through. Remove and set aside.

4. In the skillet, add in the seedless raspberry jam, orange juice and white wine vinegar. Deglaze the bottom of the skillet. Allow to come to a boil. Cook for 2 to 3 minutes or until slightly thick in consistency.

5. Spoon the sauce over the pork chops.

6. Serve with a garnish of thyme sprigs.

Recipe 15: Date Loaf Cake

This is a dish that tastes identical to date pudding, but in a bread loaf form. It is moist and incredibly easy to make.

Yield: 12 servings

Preparation Time: 1 hour and 10 minutes

Ingredient List:

- 1 cup of dates, pits removed and chopped
- 1 cup of light brown sugar
- ¼ cup of margarine
- 1 cup of water, boiling
- 1 ¾ cups of self-rising flour
- 1 teaspoon of baker's style baking soda
- 2 teaspoons of pure vanilla

HHHHHHHHHHHHHHHHHHHHHHHHHHHHHHHHHHHHHHH

Instructions:

1. Preheat the oven to 400 degrees. Grease a loaf pan and dust lightly with flour.

2. In a bowl, add in the chopped dates, light brown sugar, margarine and water. Stir well to mix. Allow to rest for 15 minutes.

3. Add in the self-rising flour, pure vanilla and baking soda. Stir well to mix.

4. Pour into the loaf pan.

5. Place into the oven to bake for 45 minutes.

6. Remove and cool for 15 minutes before serving.

Recipe 16: Anzac Biscuits

These biscuits are essential in Australian homes filled with children. They are packed full of coconut, butter and syrup, making them a perfect treat for children of all ages.

Yield: 12 servings

Preparation Time: 35 minutes

Ingredient List:

- 2 cups of rolled oats
- 2 cups of all-purpose flour
- 2 cups of coconut, flaked
- 1 ½ cup of white sugar
- 1 cup of butter
- 4 Tablespoons of gold syrup
- 1 teaspoon of baker's style baking soda
- 2 Tablespoons of water, boiling

HHHHHHHHHHHHHHHHHHHHHHHHHHHHHHHHHHHHHH

Instructions:

1. Preheat the oven to 325 degrees. Grease baking sheets with cooking spray.

2. In a bowl, add in the rolled oats, all-purpose flour, flaked coconut and white sugar. Stir well to mix.

3. In a saucepan set over medium heat, add in the butter and golden syrup. Allow to come to a simmer. Remove from heat. Add in the baking soda and water. Stir well to mix. Pour into the oat mix. Stir well until evenly blended.

4. Divide the mix into balls. Place onto the baking sheet.

5. Place into the oven to bake for 20 minutes.

6. Remove and cool for 15 minutes before serving.

Recipe 17: Sausage and Cranberry Stuffing

This is the perfect stuffing dish for you to make during your next Australian themed Thanksgiving. It is so delicious, you will want to make it every Thanksgiving.

Yield: 10 servings

Preparation Time: 1 hour and 40 minutes

Ingredient List:

- 1 ½ cups of whole wheat bread, cut into cubes
- 3 ¾ cups of white bread, cut into cubes
- 1 pound of ground turkey sausage
- 1 cup of onion, chopped
- ¾ cup of celery, chopped
- 2 ½ teaspoons of sage, dried
- 1 ½ teaspoons of rosemary, dried
- ½ teaspoons of dried thyme
- 1 golden delicious apple, cored and chopped
- ¾ cup of dried cranberries
- 1/3 cup of parsley, minced
- 1 turkey liver, cooked and chopped
- ¾ cup of turkey stock
- 4 Tablespoons of butter, melted

HHHHHHHHHHHHHHHHHHHHHHHHHHHHHHHHHHHHH

Instructions:

1. Preheat the oven to 350 degrees.

2. Spread the whole wheat and white bread cubes onto a baking sheet. Place into the oven to bake for 6 to 8 minutes or until toasted. Remove and transfer into a bowl.

3. In a skillet set over medium heat, add in the chopped onions and ground turkey sausage. Cook for 8 to 10 minutes or until browned.

4. Add in the chopped celery, dried sage, dried rosemary and dried thyme. Stir well to mix. Cook for 2 minutes.

5. Pour into the bowl with the bread cubes.

6. Add in the chopped apple, dried cranberries, minced parsley and cooked turkey liver. Stir well to mix.

7. Add in the turkey stock and melted butter. Stir well to incorporate.

8. Allow to cool before serving.

Recipe 18: Australian Soda Bread

This is the perfect bread recipe for you to serve alongside your next Australian dinner night. It is so delicious, you will want to make as often as possible.

Yield: 8 servings

Preparation Time:50 minutes

Ingredient List:

- 2 ¾ cups of all-purpose flour
- 4 ½ teaspoons of baking powder
- 1 teaspoon of salt
- 5 ½ Tablespoons of butter, cold and cut into pieces
- ¾ cup of water
- Syrup, for serving

HHHHHHHHHHHHHHHHHHHHHHHHHHHHHHHHHHHHHHH

Instructions:

1. In a bowl, add in the all-purpose flour, dash of salt and baking powder. Stir well to mix.

2. Add in the butter pieces. Cut in with a pastry cutter until crumbly in consistency.

3. Place onto a flat surface. Knead for 1 minute or until smooth in consistency.

4. Preheat the oven to 400 degrees. Place a sheet of parchment paper onto a baking sheet.

5. Roll out the dough until 7 inches in diameter. Place onto the baking sheet.

6. Dust the dough with flour and slice into 8 wedges. Dust the top with flour.

7. Place into the oven to bake for 35 to 40 minutes or until golden. Remove and set aside to cool for 5 minutes before serving.

Recipe 19: Surprise Cheddar Biscuits

These delicious cheddar biscuits are the perfect way to start off your morning. It is packed full of the essential nutrients you need in order kick off your morning the right way.

Yield: 4 servings

Preparation Time: 15 minutes

Ingredient List:

- 1 cup of all-purpose flour
- 1 tablespoon of white sugar
- 1 ½ teaspoons of baker's style baking powder
- Dash of salt
- ½ teaspoons of baker's style baking soda
- 2 Tablespoons of butter, cold and cut into pieces
- ½ cup of cheddar cheese, shredded
- 2 Tablespoons of chives, chopped
- 6 ounces of Greek yogurt
- 2 eggs

HHHHHHHHHHHHHHHHHHHHHHHHHHHHHHHHHHHHHHH

Instructions:

1. Preheat the oven to 475 degrees.

2. In a pot set over medium to high heat, fill with water. Allow to come to a boil. Add in the eggs. Boil for 5 minutes. Remove from heat and set the eggs aside.

3. In a bowl, add in the all-purpose flour, white sugar, dash of salt, baking powder and soda. Stir well to mix. Add in the cold butter. Cut in with a pastry cutter until crumbly in consistency. Add in the shredded cheddar cheese and Greek yogurt. Stir well until evenly mixed.

4. Grease a baking sheet with cooking spray.

5. Remove the hardboiled eggs from their shells.

6. Shape ¼ cup of the dough into a biscuit shape. Place onto the baking sheet. Repeat. Create a well in each of the biscuits. Place the eggs into the well facing sideways.

7. Form a second biscuit from the dough and place over the top of the egg. Repeat.

8. Place into the oven to bake for 5 minutes. Lower the heat of the oven to 400 degrees. Continue to bake for 7 to 8 minutes or until golden.

9. Drizzle melted butter over the top of the biscuits. Sprinkle the chopped chives over the top.

10. Serve.

Recipe 20: Pesto Prawns

Prawns, or shrimp, are highly popular in Australia and now once you get a taste of this dish, you will understand why.

Yield: 8 servings

Preparation Time:30 minutes

Ingredient List:

- 1 pound of linguine
- ½ cup of butter
- 2 cups of heavy whipping cream
- ½ teaspoons of black pepper
- 1 cup of grated parmesan cheese
- 1/3 cup of pesto
- 1 pound of prawns, peeled

HHHHHHHHHHHHHHHHHHHHHHHHHHHHHHHHHHHHHHH

Instructions:

1. In a pot set over medium to high heat, fill with salted water. Allow to come to a boil. Add in the linguine. Cook for 8 to 10 minutes or until soft. Drain and set aside.

2. In a skillet set over medium heat, add in the butter. Once melted, add in the heavy whipping cream. Season with a dash of salt and black pepper. Cook for 7 to 8 minutes.

3. Add in the parmesan cheese. Stir well to mix.

4. Add in the pesto. Cook for 5 minutes or until thick in consistency.

5. Add in the prawns. Continue to cook for 5 minutes or until bright pink in color. Remove from heat.

6. Serve the prawns and sauce over the cooked linguine.

Recipe 21: Australian Pavlova

This is the perfect Australian recipe to make during the hot summer months. This dish is crunchy and made in a crumbly meringue shell I know you will love.

Yield: 8 servings

Preparation Time: 2 hours

Ingredients for the meringue:

- 6 egg whites
- 1 ¾ cup of caster sugar
- 1 teaspoon of corn flour
- 1 teaspoon of vinegar
- 1 teaspoon of pure vanilla
- Ingredients for the whipped cream:
- 3 ¼ cups of heavy whipping cream
- 1/3 cup of caster sugar
- 1 teaspoon of pure vanilla

Ingredients for the toppings:

- Strawberries, sliced into halves
- 1 banana, thinly sliced
- Powdered sugar, for dusting

HHHHHHHHHHHHHHHHHHHHHHHHHHHHHHHHHHHHH

Instructions:

1. Preheat the oven to 300 degrees. Place a sheet of parchment paper onto a baking sheet.

2. In a bowl, add in the egg whites. Beat with an electric mixer for 10 minutes or until glossy.

3. Add in the vinegar and pure vanilla. Continue to beat for 1 minute.

4. Scoop circles of the meringue onto the baking sheet. Place into the oven to bake for 1 hour until crispy on the outside.

5. In a bowl, add in the heavy whipping cream. Beat with an electric mixer for 3 minutes or until fluffy in consistency. Add in the caster sugar and pure vanilla. Continue to beat until firm.

6. Scoop the whipped cream over the top of the meringue biscuits.

7. Top off with the strawberry halves and banana slices. Dust with powdered sugar.

Recipe 22: Rosemary and Cheese Dampers

This is a modern Australian classic often served in many Australian households today. It is packed full of plenty of cheese that you won't be able to resist.

Yield: 6 servings

Preparation Time: 1 hour

Ingredient List:

- 3 cups of self-rising flour
- 3 Tablespoons of butter, cut into pieces
- 1 teaspoon of baking powder
- ½ teaspoons of sea salt
- 1 ¼ cups o buttermilk
- 1 cup of grated cheddar cheese
- 1 tablespoon of extra virgin olive oil
- 1 tablespoon of rosemary leaves, chopped
- ¼ cup of grated Parmesan cheese
- Dash of salt and black pepper

HHHHHHHHHHHHHHHHHHHHHHHHHHHHHHHHHHHHH

Instructions:

1. In a food processor, add in the self-rising flour, dash of salt and baking powder. Add in the butter and pulse well until crumbly in consistency. Transfer into a bowl.

2. In the bowl, add in the buttermilk and grated cheese. Stir well to mix.

3. Place the dough onto a flat surface. Knead for 2 minutes or until soft. Divide the dough into 6 pieces. Shape into balls. Place onto a baking sheet.

4. Slice a cross shape into the top of each piece. Brush with the olive oil.

5. Sprinkle the chopped rosemary and grated Parmesan cheese over the top. Season with a dash of salt and black pepper.

6. Place into an oven to bake at 400 degrees for 20 minutes or until golden. Remove and set aside to cool for 5 minutes.

7. Serve.

Recipe 23: Australian Spinach and Strawberry Salad

This is a delicious salad dish that you can make whenever you are craving something on the lighter side. It is so delicious, I guarantee you will want to make it every chance you get.

Yield: 4 servings

Preparation Time: 1 hour and 10 minutes

Ingredient List:

- 2 Tablespoons of sesame seeds
- 1 tablespoon of poppy seeds
- ½ cup of white sugar
- ½ cup of extra virgin olive oil
- ¼ cup of white vinegar, distilled
- ¼ teaspoons of smoked paprika
- ¼ teaspoons of Worcestershire sauce
- 1 tablespoon of onion, minced
- 10 ounces of spinach, torn into pieces
- 1 quart of strawberries, thinly sliced
- ¼ cup of almonds, cut into slivers

HHHHHHHHHHHHHHHHHHHHHHHHHHHHHHHHHHHHHHH

Instructions:

1. In a bowl, add in the sesame seeds, extra virgin olive oil, distilled white vinegar, smoked paprika, Worcestershire sauce, minced onion and poppy seeds. Stir well to mix.

2. Cover and set into the fridge to chill for 1 hour.

3. In a separate bowl, add in the torn spinach, sliced strawberries and almond slivers. Toss well to mix.

4. Pour the dressing over the top. Toss to coat.

5. Cover and set into the fridge to chill for 10 to 15 minutes.

6. Serve.

Recipe 24: Fairy Bread

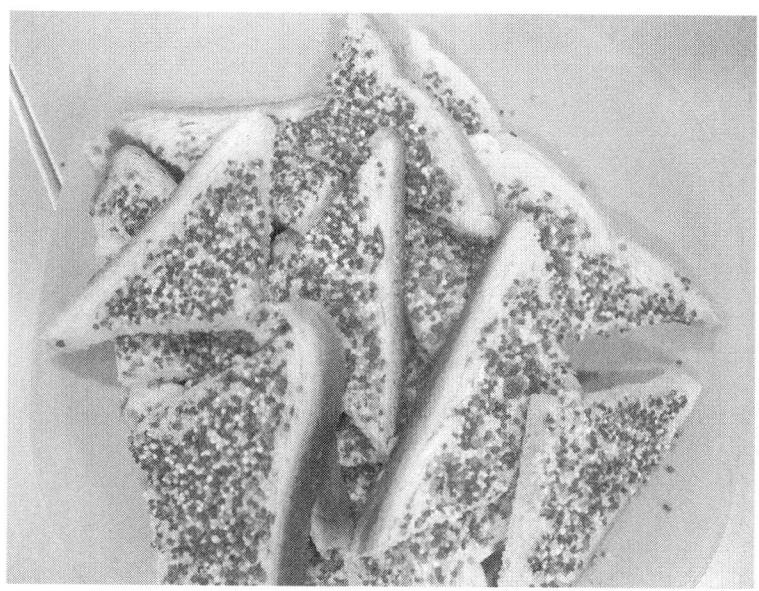

This is one of the best Australian recipes that you can make for those picky eaters in your household. Every person in your home will love it.

Yield: 2 servings

Preparation Time:5 minutes

Ingredient List:

- 4 slices of white bread
- 8 teaspoons of butter
- 8 teaspoons of rainbow sprinkles

HHHHHHHHHHHHHHHHHHHHHHHHHHHHHHHHHHHHHH

Instructions:

1. Remove the crusts from the white bread slices.

2. Spread the butter over the bread slices. Slice into triangle shapes.

3. Sprinkle the rainbow sprinkles over the top of the bread slices.

4. Serve immediately.

Recipe 25: Australian Date Pudding

This is a delicious dish that is the ultimate comfort food whenever you are feeling under the weather. Make this whenever you want to spoil yourself.

Yield: 4 servings

Preparation Time: 1 hour

Ingredients for the pudding:

- 6 1/3 ounces of dates, pits removed and chopped
- 1 ¼ cups of water
- ½ teaspoons of baking soda
- ¾ cup of light brown sugar
- ¼ cup of butter, soft
- 2 eggs
- 1 cup of self-rising flour

Ingredients for the sauce:

- 3 ½ Tablespoons of butter
- 1 cup of light brown sugar
- 1 cup of heavy whipping cream
- 1 teaspoon of pure vanilla

HHHHHHHHHHHHHHHHHHHHHHHHHHHHHHHHHHHHHH

Instructions:

1. Prepare the pudding. In a saucepan set over high heat, add in the chopped dates and water. Allow to come to a boil. Remove from heat. Add in the baking soda and stir well to mix.

2. In a bowl, add in the butter and light brown sugar. Beat with an electric mixer until smooth. Add in the eggs and continue to beat until fluffy in consistency. Add in the date mix and beat well to mix.

3. Add in the flour and stir well to incorporate.

4. Pour the mix into 8 pudding molds, making sure to fill each 2/3 of the way full. Transfer the molds into a baking dish.

5. Place into the oven to bake at 355 degrees for 40 minutes or until golden. Remove and set aside.

6. Prepare the sauce. In a saucepan set over low heat, add in the butter, light brown sugar, heavy whipping cream and pure vanilla. Allow to come to a boil. Cook for 5 minutes or until the sauce is thick in consistency.

7. Invert the pudding onto a serving plate. Drizzle the sauce over the top.

8. Serve.

About the Author

Angel Burns learned to cook when she worked in the local seafood restaurant near her home in Hyannis Port in Massachusetts as a teenager. The head chef took Angel under his wing and taught the young woman the tricks of the trade for cooking seafood. The skills she had learned at a young age helped her get accepted into Boston University's Culinary Program where she also minored in business administration.

Summers off from school meant working at the same restaurant but when Angel's mentor and friend retired as head chef, she took over after graduation and created classic and new dishes that delighted the diners. The restaurant flourished under Angel's culinary creativity and one customer developed more than an appreciation for Angel's food. Several months after taking over the position, the young woman met her future husband at work and they have been inseparable ever since. They still live in Hyannis Port with their two children and a cocker spaniel named Buddy.

Angel Burns turned her passion for cooking and her business acumen into a thriving e-book business. She has authored several successful books on cooking different types of dishes using simple ingredients for novices and experienced chefs alike. She is still head chef in Hyannis Port and says she will probably never leave!

Author's Afterthoughts

With so many books out there to choose from, I want to thank you for choosing this one and taking precious time out of your life to buy and read my work. Readers like you are the reason I take such passion in creating these books.

It is with gratitude and humility that I express how honored I am to become a part of your life and I hope that you take the same pleasure in reading this book as I did in writing it.

Can I ask one small favour? I ask that you write an honest and open review on Amazon of what you thought of the book. This will help other readers make an informed choice on whether to buy this book.

My sincerest thanks,

Angel Burns

If you want to be the first to know about news, new books, events and giveaways, subscribe to my newsletter by clicking the link below

https://angel-burns.gr8.com

or Scan QR-code

Printed in Great Britain
by Amazon